TO

FROM

Design: Tim Steele
Editing: Michelle Sedas

Printed and bound in the United States of America by
Pinnacle Press, Inc.
St. Louis, Missouri

ISBN No. 1-933310-98-7

www.dynamicapproach.com
www.lauriecalzada.com

INSPIRING PASSION IN OTHERS

BY LAURIE CALZADA

ACKNOWLEDGEMENTS

Mac Anderson and Eric Harvey.
You both believed in me at moments
I didn't believe in myself.

All my thanks to Tim Steele.
You have inspired me along
this exciting journey.

A very special thanks to
Kathy Freely and Charlotte Pugh.
You stood by me and brightened my life
in moments of darkness and uncertainty.

To William Camp.
Thank you for the "unknown inspiration."
The brief moment of our paths crossing
truly changed my life forever.
I will be indebted to you for an eternity.

INTRODUCTION

The smallest words and the tiniest lessons in life often have the greatest impact. On a late September evening, two words were spoken by one man that changed my life forever.

During a business trip with executives of A.G. Edwards, I had a gentleman who repeatedly told me how much "passion" I had in life, and how "inspired" he was by observing me. He stated that he only wished more people had that sort of passion in life. For months, those words filled my mind on a daily basis. Little did he know the challenges that I was facing in my own life, both personally and professionally. Three months later, I woke up in the wee hours of a December morning with a very heavy heart...not knowing...not understanding...not comprehending...why I was floating in a sea of chaos, uncertainty and unhappiness. In this pinnacle moment, I realized how many times over the past year I had focused on "I" and "me," instead of focusing on "you" and "we." I had come to a point in life where I had no hopes, no dreams, no aspirations, and most importantly, I had lost my passion. As I lay there staring into darkness, I realized that a life without passion is like a darkened room. I took pen to paper, and over the next hour I wrote *Inspiring Passion in Others*.

Here was a man who entered my life for a brief moment in time, and he was looking from the outside-in...seeing a person filled with joy, inspiration and passion. However, I was looking from the inside-out...seeing the emptiness, heartache, loneliness and doubt.

As we continue on our journey of life, we need to: laugh more and cry less; spend more time with those that mean the most; not wait for tomorrow to correct what we can today; learn to say we're sorry instead of saying we're right; and treasure every moment in time.

Everything we do, and everything we say, leaves a fingerprint on someone's life forever. Remember to live your life to the fullest, embrace the opportunities you are given, spend time with those that mean the most in your life, and remember that what you do will always have an impact on other people's lives, whether positive or negative.

The passion that lies within you must be discovered. Many people give up on their dreams, and they lose their passion, because they feel that it's too late. Remember that it is never too late to find your passion and to live your dreams. So many times in life people look back and say, "I wish I could have...should have...would have..." While you cannot change the past, you can mold your future. Therefore, stop dreaming about tomorrow, and start living for today. Dreams are not just for dreaming—they are for living.

> *Our dreams may not come true in the time frame that we desire, but they will be in the time frame that was designed.*

We should all have one ultimate goal in life. When we stand at the pearly gates, may God look down and say, "Well done my good and faithful servant."

Remember to live your life with true passion,

Laurie Cazada

INSPIRING PASSION
IN OTHERS

BY LAURIE CALZADA

I SIT STARING INTO
DARKNESS,
WONDERING WHAT
MIGHT HAVE BEEN.

I MISSED THE KEY INGREDIENT... MY PASSION THAT LIES WITHIN.

BECOMING
OVERWHELMED
BY ALL MY
THOUGHTS AND FEARS,

INSTEAD OF **FOCUSING** ON
WHAT **MATTERS MOST**,
THE **JOY** IN ALL MY YEARS.

I SPEND SO MUCH TIME

WORRYING

ABOUT THE PETTY THINGS.

WOULDN'T MY ENERGY
BE BETTER SPENT
EMBRACING OTHERS'
DREAMS?

As I REFLECT ON THE
LIFE I LEAD, I NEED TO
STOP AND THINK.

IT MATTERS NOT
WHAT I HAVE DONE,
BUT THOSE THAT I HAVE
REACHED.

IT BECOMES SO EASY TO
PONDER
ALL THAT I HAVE
MISSED.

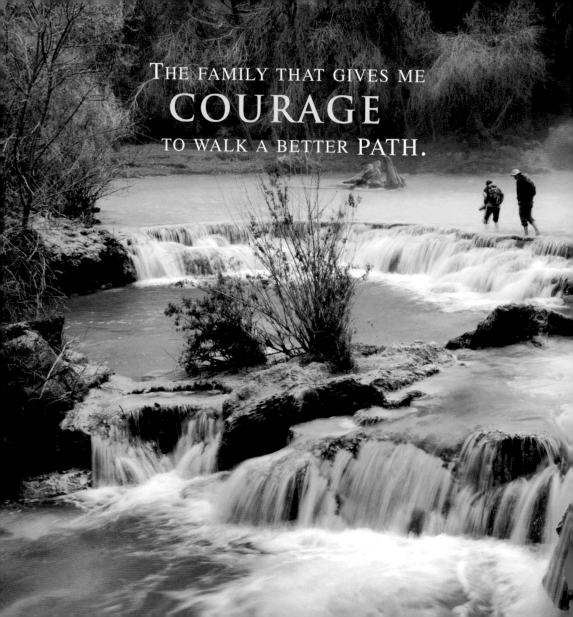

THE FAMILY THAT GIVES ME
COURAGE
TO WALK A BETTER PATH.

THE CHILDREN
THAT FILL MY HEART
WITH EVERY PASSING
BREATH.

THE LAUGHTER THAT
SURROUNDS ME
FROM ALL MY TREASURED
FRIENDS.

THE **INSPIRATION**
THAT OTHERS GIVE
TO SEEK THE **BETTER END.**

SHOULDN'T I
EMBRACE TODAY
WITH ALL MY
JOYOUS MIGHT?

TOMORROW MIGHT
BECOME THE DAY
I CANNOT MAKE THINGS
RIGHT.

FOR TODAY IS
BUT A GLIMPSE
OF WHAT MY
PRESENCE IS.

I OFTEN LOOK BEHIND ME TO IMAGINE WHAT COULD HAVE BEEN.

INSPIRATION IS
HAVING STRENGTH
TO LOOK BEYOND
MY OWN DESIRES.

BEING ABLE TO
FOCUS ON OTHERS,
WHO SEEK TO BE
INSPIRED.

THERE ARE MOMENTS
I CHOOSE TO FOCUS
ON ME INSTEAD OF YOU.

THOSE **MOMENTS** IN MY
LIFE REVEAL I
LOST WHAT IS SO TRUE.

THERE ARE MOMENTS
I BEGIN TO **FOCUS**
ON **YOU** INSTEAD OF **ME.**

That's when
life begins to SHOW
what's really
MEANT TO BE.

WHEN MY FINAL DAYS
APPROACH ME
IN THE VERY END,

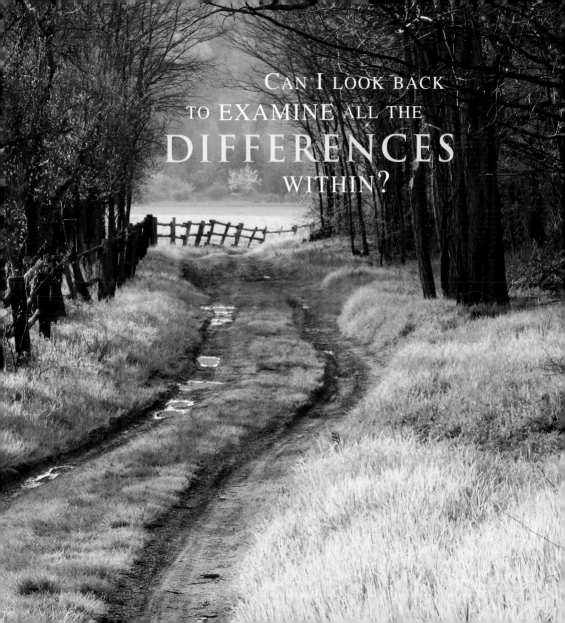

CAN I LOOK BACK
TO EXAMINE ALL THE
DIFFERENCES
WITHIN?

My life should be an

INSPIRATION

FROM THE VERY START.

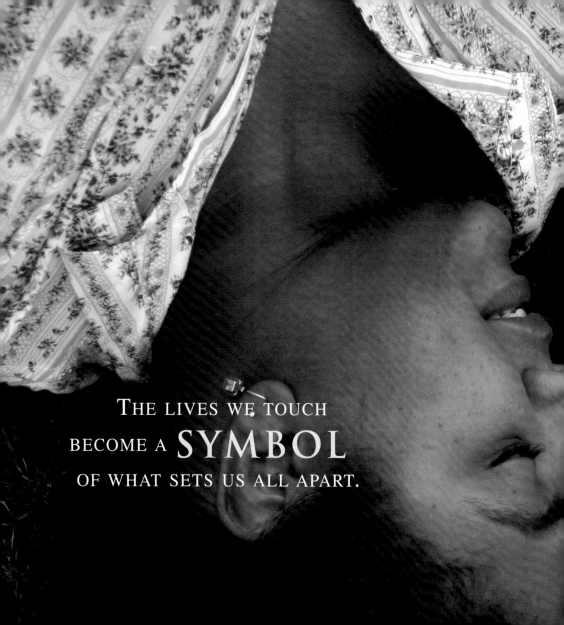

THE LIVES WE TOUCH
BECOME A SYMBOL
OF WHAT SETS US ALL APART.

MANY DAYS I FOCUS ON
DREAMING,
INSTEAD OF **LIVING**
MY DESIRES.

I forget what
life is ALL ABOUT,
and how I can
INSPIRE.

As I walk into a
FUTURE
THAT LOOKS EXCITING
AND SO BRIGHT,

I HOPE TO REMEMBER

THOSE WHO

HELP ME TO DO

WHAT'S RIGHT.

WITH THE GIFTS
THAT I'VE BEEN GIVEN,
I SHALL LIVE MY LIFE
FOR OTHERS.

INSPIRING ALL
THEY WANT TO BE,
SHOWING THAT PASSION
YOU CANNOT COVER.

THAT IS FILLED WITH MUCH DESPAIR.

BUT WITH THE
STRENGTH
I GAIN TODAY,
I WILL MEET IT
WELL-PREPARED.

So as I sit here
IN THE DARKNESS,
FILLED WITH PASSION
IN MY HEART,

I REMEMBER
WHAT MATTERS MOST…
THE INSPIRATION
I HAVE SET APART.

WHEN ALL THE
SHADOWS FADE,
AND THE SUN BEGINS
TO BEAM,

ALL I WANT TO
HOLD SO DEAR,
ARE THOSE THAT FULFILL
MY DREAMS...

DEDICATION

This book is dedicated to
Angeles and Austin.
You help me to live my life
with great passion every day.

ABOUT THE AUTHOR

Laurie Calzada is an entrepreneur, author, motivational speaker and trainer with 20 years of experience. She presents on many topics such as finding your passion, leadership, mastering change and sales.

Her focus is to motivate those that have a desire to excel, and her life has proven that you can accomplish anything with enough determination and ambition. Her outstanding career has allowed her to consult and present for hundreds of Fortune 1,000 companies.

With an entrepreneurial spirit, she has successfully owned and founded seven different start-up operations over the past 20 years. Currently, she owns three companies, and travels internationally to speak to organizations. Laurie brings a contagious enthusiasm to all the lives she touches, and she truly has found her passion in life.

Ms. Calzada began her career 20 years ago while studying Marketing at the University of Maryland, European Division in Oxford, England. In addition, she received a certificate of Broadcast Journalism from the Broadcast Center.

For more information, visit Laurie's website at **www.lauriecalzada.com**.

NINE PRINCIPLES
TO LIVING YOUR LIFE WITH PASSION

by Laurie Calzada
Coming 2007

This powerful book is based on a speech that Ms. Calzada wrote in 2006. Since the speech has impacted so many lives, she was led to write a book on The Nine Principles.

The book starts with **Principle #1: Discover Your Passion,** and leads you through all aspects of life in dealing with yourself, other people and life's circumstances. By the time you finish reading **Principle #9: Unlock Your Passion,** you will realize that you must find your destiny in life, and you will never fully live your life until you have found your passion.

Once again, using her own personal experience when she felt that life had left her without any hopes or dreams, she touches your life as a person, as a parent, as a leader, and as a friend.